Dream Doll

Purple hair is not as unusual as it used to be. This dreamy doll is fun to make. She can also be worn as a pin. Dress her in colors to match a season or your personal attire.

FINISHED SIZE: 4" tall

MATERIALS:
Fabric • Lightweight cardboard • *Aleene's* Tacky glue • Wood ice cream spoon • 22 gauge wire • Pipe cleaners • Decorative yarns • Black *StazOn* ink pad • *JudiKins* face cube stamp #9522 • Red Liner tape • *Prismacolor* pencils • Beads (alphabet, tiny no-hole) • Optional pin back

INSTRUCTIONS:

Make body: Trace body pattern onto lightweight cardboard. Cut out. • Glue handle of spoon to wide end of cardboard body. • Cut 14" colored wire. • Cut 7" square of fabric. Fold diagonally. • Tuck body between layers. Fold outside points (B & C) to point A. • Adjust cardboard/spoon and gather fabric around neck area. • Place center of wire at gathered area. Wrap around neck several times to secure fabric. • Trim away excess fabric covering spoon. • Leave the ends of the wire long; you will use them later.

Make arms: Lay 2 pipe cleaners side by side. Cut 2 inches off one end. Twist pipe cleaners together, then fold in half. • Cut fabric 2" x 7". • Lay fabric on table wrong side up. Squeeze line of glue along one edge of fabric. Lay twisted pipe cleaners on top of glue. • Dab glue on each end of fabric. Fold ends of fabric towards center. • Tightly roll fabric and pipe cleaner, making a "log" with pipe cleaner inside rolled fabric. Squeeze a line of glue along edge of fabric to secure. • Center arms behind neck. Using wires at neck, wrap wire around each arm. At the end, wind wire tight and close together for hand. Tuck in wire ends.

Chest: Cut fabric 1" x 8". • Center at back of neck, wrapping fabric in an "x" pattern across chest. Secure with glue. • Cut 12" of fancy yarn. Wrap around bodice and neck area. Tie at back. Glue a scrap of decorative fabric on front of body. •

Face: Stamp face onto 2" circle of muslin fabric with Black ink. • Color face with pencils. • Place Red liner tape on back of face. • Cut out face shape (wider at forehead, narrower at chin). • Peel off other side of tape and set aside. • Adhere Red liner tape to wooden spoon in face area. • Peel paper off tape. Place fabric face in center (tape side to tape side). • Pour tiny no-hole beads onto exposed areas of tape.

Hair: Cut 24" of fancy fiber. • Wrap around 5" square of cardboard, slide off end. Tie a knot in the center, keeping loops in the ends of the yarn. • Glue hair to back of head.

Finishing: Cut wire 8" long. String "Dream" letter beads on wire. Lay across chest and twist at back to secure wire. • Stitch pin on back of doll if desired.

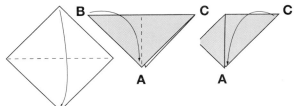

"Silly Girl" Pins

Silly Girl pins are easy to make. Write names on the dresses before shrinking to make fun name tags. Wouldn't they be great for a bridal shower? These girls would add a bit of whimsy to those "Girl's Night Out" scrapbook pages.

The combinations of colors and stamped designs provide endless creative adventures.

FINISHED SIZE: 4½" tall

MATERIALS:
White artist quality shrink plastic • *Crafter's* ink pads • *Prismacolor* pencils or chalk pastels • Rubber stamps • *Pigma* Micron .005 Black pen • 22-24 gauge colored wire • Beads (bugle, seed) • ⅛" hole punch • Pencil • Very fine sanding block • *Krylon* fixative • E6000 • Bar pin back

MATERIALS USED TO DRAW FACE:
Pigma Micron .005 pens (Brown, Black) • *Pentel* Milky White gel roller pen • *Prismacolor* pencils (True Blue, Violet, Crème, Light Peach, Blush Pink, Scarlet Lake, Apple Green, Sienna Brown)

TIPS: **Shrink Plastic**: *Pencil lines on shrink plastic must be trimmed off before heating or they become heavy and dark.* • *Holes must be punched in shrink plastic before heating.* • **Face**: *Eyes are about halfway down the face.* • *Use only Brown pen to draw features. Add touches of Black to eyebrows and eyelashes only.* • *Use a light touch and go over lines several times until you are satisfied with the results.* • *Put the Black pupil and White highlight in eyes. Both give eyes "life".* • *Place pupils so doll is looking a little down and to the left. Placing pupils right in the center of the eye creates a staring lifeless expression.* • *This is a cartoon face, don't worry if the eyes aren't exactly the same or if the nose is a little crooked. It isn't supposed to look like a real person!*

INSTRUCTIONS:
Prepare Plastic: Lightly sand both sides. To shrink plastic evenly, sand in both directions • Use pencil to trace pattern onto shrink plastic. Cut it out, trimming away pencil line. • Punch ⅛" holes where indicated. • Decorate shrink plastic using Crafter's ink, colored pencils, or chalk pastels. Apply chalks with fingertips. Colors become much darker after plastic shrinks, so use lightly. • Stamp desired designs on dress after applying chalks.

Draw face: Use .005 pen in Brown and Black. • See Tips for drawing faces.

Shrink Plastic: Follow manufacturer's directions to shrink plastic. Remove from oven when piece becomes flat. Let cool.

Necklace: Cut 6" wire. • Slide 4 seed beads onto center of wire. Place beads against front of neck. • Bend wires towards back of neck. Cross wires in back and insert right wire in left arm hole. Insert left wire into right arm hole. The wire will be sticking out through the front and both ends should be the same length.

Arms: String seed beads on wires. Make tight coil to hold beads one inch from end of wire. • Add a charm or purse by stringing wire through coil at end of arm (Think of it as a hand). Bend arms at elbow to give her

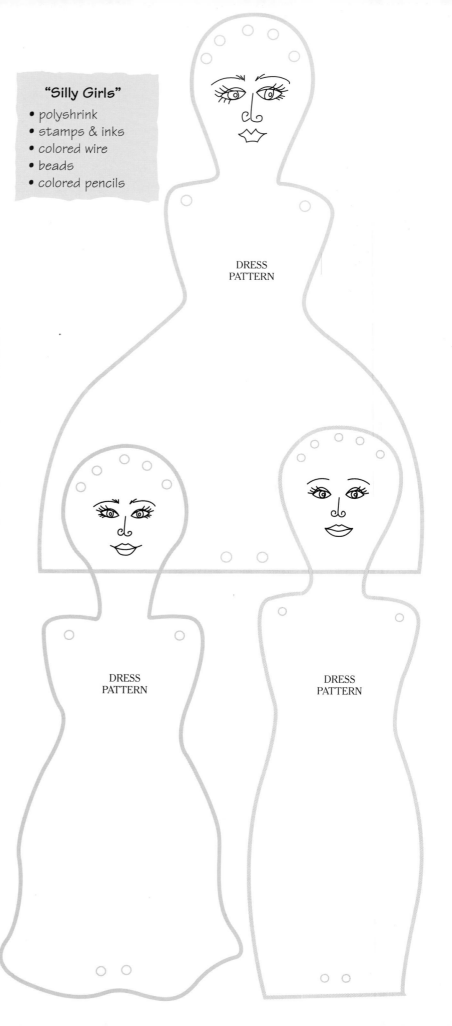

"Silly Girls"
• polyshrink
• stamps & inks
• colored wire
• beads
• colored pencils

DRESS PATTERN

DRESS PATTERN

DRESS PATTERN

that sassy "hands on hip" look.

Legs: Cut 5" wire. • From back, insert ends of wire into holes punched for legs. String beads on wires. • Make a tight coil to hold beads on 1" from end of wire.

Feet: Fold last 1/4" of leg at a right angle.

Hair: Cut 24" colored wire. • Loop wire through holes at top of head. Make coils for hair. • Add seed beads to wire and make a small tight loop to keep it in place. • Use two 24" pieces of wire for more curls.

Finishing: Lightly spray front of pin with Krylon fixative so colors will not rub off. Attach pin back with E-6000 glue. Let dry.

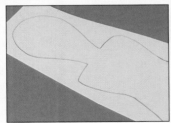

1. Trace pattern on plastic.

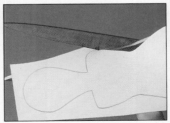

2. Cut out pattern inside line.

3. Color the plastic.

4. Stamp dress.

5. Draw face.

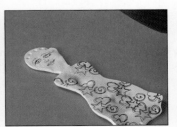

6. Heat and shrink.

Angels

These Angels make wonderful gifts for all ages. Add a loop hanger for a lovely holiday ornament.

Personalize your angel with Bible verses or a name on the dress. Remember that the writing is going to become very tiny after shrinking.

FINISHED SIZE: 5" tall

BASIC MATERIALS:
White artist quality shrink plastic • *Crafter's* ink pads • *Prismacolor* pencils or chalk pastels • *Hero Arts* star stamps • *Pigma* Micron .005 Black pen • 22-24 gauge colored wire • Beads (bugle, seed) • Pencil • Very fine sanding block • 1/8" hole punch • *Krylon* fixative • E6000 • Bar pin back

MATERIALS USED TO DRAW FACE: *Pigma* Micron .005 pens (Brown, Black) • *Pentel* Milky White gel roller pen • *Prismacolor* pencils (True Blue, Violet, Crème, Light Peach, Blush Pink, Scarlet Lake, Apple Green, Sienna Brown)

TIPS: **Shrink Plastic:** *Pencil lines on shrink plastic must be trimmed off before heating or they become heavy and dark. • Holes must be punched in shrink plastic before heating.*
Eace: *Eyes are about halfway down the face. • Use only Brown pen to draw features. Add touches of Black to eyebrows and eyelashes only. • Use a light touch and go over lines several times until you are satisfied with the results. • Put the Black pupil and White highlight in eyes. Both give eyes "life". • Place pupils so doll is looking a little down and to the left. Placing pupils right in the center of the eye creates a staring lifeless expression. • This is a cartoon face, don't worry if the eyes aren't exactly the same or if the nose is a little crooked. It isn't supposed to look like a real person!*
Holding objects: *Your angel can hold things, like stars and hearts. Punch a hole in the hand before shrinking so you can attach the things you want her to hold.*

DRESS PATTERN

BASIC INSTRUCTIONS:
Prepare Plastic: Lightly sand both sides of shrink plastic in both directions to shrink plastic evenly. • Use pencil to trace pattern onto shrink plastic. • Cut 2 upper sleeves, 2 lower arms, wings, and body, trimming away pencil line. • Punch 1/8" holes where indicated. • Decorate shrink plastic using Crafter's ink, colored pencils, or chalk pastels. Apply chalks with fingertips. Colors become much darker after plastic shrinks, so use lightly. • Stamp designs on dress after applying chalks.
Draw face: Use .005 pen in Brown and Black. • See Tips for drawing faces.

Shrink Plastic: Follow manufacturer's directions to shrink plastic. Remove from oven when piece becomes flat. Let cool.
Hair: Cut 24" colored wire. • Loop wire through holes at top of head. Make coils for hair. • Use 2 wires 24" long for more curls.
Arms: Color and stamp upper sleeves to match dress. • Color lower arms in skin tone. • Shrink pieces.
Finishing: Lightly spray front of pin with Krylon fixative so colors will not rub off.

ARM
PATTERN
(Cut 2)

UPPER
SLEEVE
PATTERN
(Cut 2)

WINGS PATTERN

Yellow Angel

INSTRUCTIONS:

Feet: Cut 2 wires 3" long. Thread 1 wire through hole in bottom of skirt. Fold wire. Thread both ends through bead. Coil each end. Repeat for other foot.

Arms: Cut 4 wires 1" long. Align holes in arm and sleeve. Thread wire through hole. Coil end at shoulder at front and back. Repeat steps at elbow. Repeat for other arm.

Wings: Cut 2 wires 3" long. • Align holes in neck and wings. • Thread through from front. Twist ends in back.

Beads: Cut 5" wire. Coil one end tightly. Thread through hand from front. Add beads. Wrap around shoulder, thread out thru bead, then thru hole in other hand. Coil end tightly.

HEART
PATTERN

Blue Angel

INSTRUCTIONS:

Feet: Cut 3" wire. Insert into hole. Make small coil in front. Slide on 1/2" of beads. Make small coil at end of wire to hold beads.

Arms: Attach lower arm to sleeve with 1" of wire. Coil front and back. • Attach upper sleeve to shoulder bringing both coils to front.

Wings: Cut 2 wires 3" long. • Align holes in neck and wings. • Thread through from back. Coil ends to make necklace.

Heart: Cut wire 2" long. Align hole in heart and hand. Thread wire through holes. Coil wire on both sides. • Glue bottom of heart to dress.

1. Wire upper arm to body.

2. Wire lower arm to upper arm.

3. Wire wings to body.

Polyshrink Angels

- polyshrink
- stamps & ink
- chalks
- wire, beads
- Sharpie marker

Sweet Potato Mini Doll Pins

A grouping of sweet potato dolls, in a variety of colors, look adorable tucked into a basket. They make a great centerpiece, then everyone at the table gets to take one home as a party favor.

Tips for Drawing the Face

Eyes are about halfway down the face.

Use a Brown pen to draw features.

Add touches of Black to eyebrows and eyelashes only. Use a light touch and go over the lines several times until satisfied with results.

Black pupil and White highlight in eyes give the eyes "life". Place pupils so doll is looking a little down and left. Placing pupils center creates a staring lifeless expression.

This is a cartoon face, don't worry if the eyes aren't exactly the same or if the nose is a little crooked. It isn't supposed to look like a real person.

FINISHED SIZE: 3" tall

MATERIALS:

8" x 10" muslin • Fabric scraps • Fibers • 11" x 11" tulle • Lightweight cardboard • *Pigma* Micron .005 pens (Brown, Black) • Decorative sewing machine threads • 22-24 gauge wire • Beads (large glass, seed, no-hole) • *Poly-fil* stuffing • *Pentel* Milky White gel roller pen• *Prismacolor* pencils (True Blue, Violet, Crème, Light Peach, Blush Pink, Scarlet Lake, Apple Green, Sienna Brown) • Crystal glitter • GOOP glue • Red Liner tape • *Paula Best* Face cube rubber stamp has 4 great faces (*Paula Best Rubber Stamps*, 831-632-0587, Moss Landing, CA)

INSTRUCTIONS:

To make collage fabric for Doll Body: Cut fabric scraps into irregularly shaped triangles and rectangles. Cover muslin base with scraps, overlapping edges 1/4". Be careful not to build up too many overlapping edges in the same place. Lay some decorative fibers across the top. • Cover whole piece with coordinating color of fine tulle. Pin every overlapping edge before moving layered piece to sewing machine.

Sewing: Drop feed dogs and install darning foot. • Starting in middle of fabric, use free-motion to stitch layers together. • Move fabric with your hands in a meandering pattern, across collage. Remove pins as you come to them. Make wiggly stitches over all overlapping edges. Use decorative rayon or variegated threads for more interest.

Pressing: Lay collage on ironing board. Place muslin on top to keep tulle from melting. Using a hot steam iron, press piece flat.

To make Doll: Trace pattern onto wrong side of collaged fabric. • Stitch on pattern line, leaving 2" opening in seam for turning. • Cut out doll, leaving a 1/4" seam allowance. Clip curves and turn right side out. • Stuff body firmly and stitch closed.

Face: Stamp face on muslin fabric, color with pencils. • Cut out face. Cut cardboard 1/8" larger than face shape. Color edge of cardboard to match fabric. Cover cardboard with Red Liner tape. Remove liner and center face on cardboard. Sprinkle no-hole beads around face edge. • When face is fin-

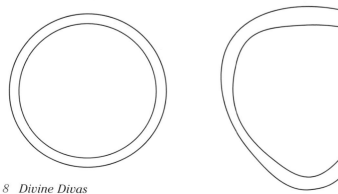

BODY
PATTERN A
Cut 2
Add a $^1/_4$"
seam allowance

BODY
PATTERN B
Cut 2
Add a $^1/_4$"
seam allowance

ished apply light layer of crystal glitter.

Attach head: Glue head to body with GOOP.

Hair: Wrap yarn around a 5" strip of cardboard. Slide off end. Tie overhand knot in center. Glue to back of head.

Arms: Cut a 5" piece of 18 gauge wire for each arm. Spiral end of wire. Add 2 large decorative beads. Make loop for elbow. Add another bead or two. Make coil for hand. Sew to doll body with double thread.

Pin: Sew pin back to doll.

Sweet Potato Doll

FINISHED SIZE: 5$^1/_2$" tall

see pattern and instructions on pages 10 - 11

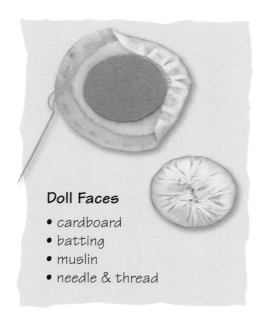

Doll Faces
- cardboard
- batting
- muslin
- needle & thread

BLUE DOLL FACE

RED DOLL FACE (page 9)

BODY PATTERN
Cut 2
Add a $1/4''$
seam allowance

Sweet Potato Dolls

Tips for Drawing the Face

Eyes are about halfway down the face.

Use a Brown pen to draw features.

Add touches of Black to eyebrows and eyelashes only. Use a light touch and go over the lines several times until satisfied with results.

Black pupil and White highlight in eyes give the eyes "life". Place pupils so doll is looking a little down and left. Placing pupils center creates a staring lifeless expression.

This is a cartoon face, don't worry if the eyes aren't exactly the same or if the nose is a little crooked. It isn't supposed to look like a real person.

1. Cover muslin with fabric scraps.

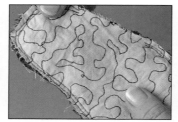

2. With right sides together, sew edges leaving an opening. Cut out body from collaged fabric.

3. Turn doll right side out and stuff.

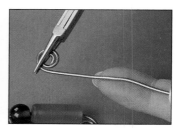

4. Shape wire arms.

5. Trace face.

6. Color face.

7. Cover a cardboard circle with batting. Gather face fabric around cardboard.

8. Picot bead the edge of face.

FINISHED SIZE: 5 1/2" tall

MATERIALS:
8" x 10" muslin • Fabric scraps • Fibers • 11" x 11" tulle • Lightweight cardboard • *Pigma* Micron .005 pens (Brown, Black) • Decorative sewing machine threads • 18 gauge wire • Beads (Large glass, seed) • Silamide or Nymo beading thread • Beading needle • *Poly-fil* stuffing • *Pentel* Milky White gel roller pen • *Prismacolor* pencils (True Blue, Violet, Crème, Light Peach, Blush Pink, Scarlet Lake, Apple Green, Sienna Brown) • Crystal glitter.

INSTRUCTIONS:

To make collage fabric for Doll Body: Cut fabric scraps into irregularly shaped triangles and rectangles. Cover muslin base with scraps, overlapping edges 1/4". Be careful not to build up too many overlapping edges in the same place. Lay some decorative fibers across the top. • Cover whole piece with coordinating color of fine tulle. Pin every overlapping edge before moving layered piece to sewing machine.

Sewing: Drop feed dogs and install darning foot. • Starting in middle of fabric, use free-motion to stitch layers together. • Move fabric with your hands in a meandering pattern, across collage. Remove pins as you come to them. Make wiggly stitches over all overlapping edges. Use decorative rayon or variegated threads for more interest.

Pressing: Lay collage on ironing board. Place muslin on top to keep tulle from melting. Using a hot steam iron, press piece flat.

To make Doll: With right sides together, trace pattern onto wrong side of fabric. • Stitch on pattern line, leaving 2" opening in seam for turning. • Cut out doll, leaving a 1/4" seam allowance. Clip curves and turn right side out. • Stuff body firmly and stitch closed.

Face: Cut a 2 1/2" circle of muslin, a 1 3/4" circle of quilt batting, and a 1 1/4" circle of cardboard. Layer muslin over batting and center both on cardboard circle. • Make Running stitches around edge of muslin. Pull thread snug, so muslin and batting are drawn tightly around edge of circle. • Make several stitches across back of circle. •

rawing face: See tips for drawing faces. Use Brown pen to draw face. Add touches of Black to eyebrows and eyelashes. • Draw Black pupil and White highlight in eyes to give eyes "life". Place pupils so the doll is looking down and left. • When face is finished, apply a light layer of a crystal glitter.

Fabric: Cut 2 1/4" circle with face centered. Cut 2" circle of quilt batting, and 1 1/4" circle of cardboard. • Layer muslin over batting and center both on cardboard circle. • Make Running stitches around edge of muslin, just inside raw edge. Pull thread snug, so muslin and batting are drawn tightly around edge of cardboard circle. • Make a few stitches in back to secure thread end. • When face is finished apply light layer of crystal glitter. •

Beading around the face: Bead around the face following the Picot Stitch and Lacy Picot Stitch instructions. •

Hair: Wrap yarn around a 5" strip of cardboard. Slide off end. Tie overhand knot in center. Stitch to back of head.

Arms: Cut a 5" piece of 18 gauge wire for each arm. Spiral end of wire. Add 2 large decorative beads. Make loop for elbow. Add another bead or two. Make coil for hand. Sew to doll body with double thread.

How to Make a Picot Stitch

Picot Stitch: Thread beading needle with beading thread. Make a few stitches in back of head to secure and bring needle out in the edge. Put 3 seed beads on needle and go down through edge. Bring thread back out bead through #3. Add 2 beads to needle. Go through edge to secure. Continue around face to beginning.

Lacy Picot Stitch: Bring thread out through beads #1 & #2. Add 4 beads. Go down through beads #6 & #7 into edge. Come back out through beads #5 & #6. Add 4 beads. Go down through beads #10 & #11 into edge. Bring thread out through beads #9 & #10. Continue around face to beginning. Knot thread on back.

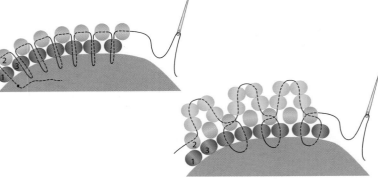

Film Can Fran and Her Sister Jan

Make these colorful dolls from scraps in your sewing room and empty film cans. Have fun choosing game pieces for legs and feet.

FINISHED SIZE: 5" & 6¼" tall

BASIC MATERIALS:
Film container • Fabric • Muslin • Buttons • Fibers • Beads • *Jacquard* Lumiere paint • Red Liner tape • *Aleene's* Tacky glue • Silamide or Nymo beading thread • Beading needle • Sewing needle and thread • Quilt batting • Cardboard

DOLL FACE

MATERIALS USED TO DRAW FACE:
Pigma Micron .005 pens (Brown, Black) • *Pentel* Milky White gel roller pen • *Prismacolor* pencils (True Blue, Violet, Crème, Light Peach, Blush Pink, Scarlet Lake, Apple Green, Sienna Brown) • Crystal glitter

INSTRUCTIONS:
Cover outside of empty film container with Red Liner tape. Measure film container. Cut fabric ½" larger on both the length and width. Remove outer layer on Red Liner tape. Align fabric with bottom edge of film container. Secure overlapping fabric edge with glue. Tuck the remaining fabric into the open end of the container. Paint container lid with Lumiere paint.

Face: Cut a 2½" circle of muslin, a 1¾" circle of quilt batting, and a 1¼" circle of cardboard. Layer muslin over batting and center both on cardboard circle. • Make Running stitches around edge of muslin. Pull thread snug, so muslin and batting are drawn tightly around edge of circle. • Make several stitches across back of circle.

Drawing face: See tips for drawing faces. Use Brown pen to draw face. Add touches of Black to eyebrows and eyelashes. • Draw Black pupil and White highlight in eyes to give eyes "life". Place pupils so the doll is looking down and left. • When face is finished, apply a light layer of a crystal glitter.

Picot stitch beading around face:

Finish: Glue buttons on body. Wrap fibers around neck.

How to Make a Picot Stitch

Picot Stitch: Thread beading needle with beading thread. Make a few stitches in back of head to secure and bring needle out in the edge. Put 3 seed beads on needle and go down through edge. Bring thread back out bead through #3. Add 2 beads to needle. Go through edge to secure. Continue around face to beginning.

Lacy Picot Stitch: Bring thread out through beads #1 & #2. Add 4 beads. Go down through beads #6 & #7 into edge. Come back out through beads #5 & #6. Add 4 beads. Go down through beads #10 & #11 into edge. Bring thread out through beads #9 & #10. Continue around face to beginning. Knot thread on back.

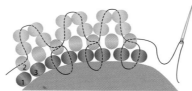

Film Can Fran & Her Sister Jan

Made on film containers for Kodak Advantix film.

Techniques:
• attaching fabric to firm surface using red liner tape
• using roll-up beads for arms & legs
• using game pieces for feet and legs
• another use for a bead framed face
• green doll uses Lumiere to cover exposed plastic edges.

Fran (green)

MATERIALS: 2 dice   FINISHED SIZE: 5" tall

INSTRUCTIONS:
Container lid is bottom of doll body.

Make fabric beads for arms, legs, neck: Cut drinking straw into 1" pieces. Cut 5 fabric strips 1¼" x 3". Glue straw to end of fabric. Roll fabric around straw and secure other end with glue. Make 2 arms, 2 legs, and 1 neck.

Assemble arms: Cut 2 pipe cleaners 2" long. • Place large glass bead on end of pipe cleaner. Make small coil to secure bead. • Place arm over pipe cleaner. • Poke holes into film container in "shoulder" area. Insert end of pipe cleaner into hole. Coil end of pipe cleaner inside film container to secure. • Repeat for other arm.

Assemble legs: Drill hole into one side of 2 dice. • Cut 2 pipe cleaners 2" long. • Glue each pipe cleaner into hole in dice. Place leg over pipe cleaner. • Make 2 holes in film container lid with awl. • Insert ends of pipe cleaner into holes. Coil ends of pipe cleaner to secure. • Place lid on film container.

Assemble neck: Cut 2" pipe cleaner. Poke hole in center bottom of container. Dip one end of pipe cleaner into glue. Insert into hole in container. Coil end to secure. Place neck bead over pipe cleaner. • Glue head to exposed end of pipe cleaner. Glue lace scrap on back of head for hair.

Jan (purple)

MATERIALS: Game pieces   FINISHED SIZE: 6¼" tall

INSTRUCTIONS:
Legs: Glue game pieces to lid.

Arms: Cut 2 pieces of 22 gauge wire 6" long. • Fold 1 in half, then wrap with fuzzy yarn. Fold and twist wire/yarn until arm is 2" long. • Poke hole in side of film container and insert end of arm into hole. Bend over end of wire inside can. • Glue buttons to front of body and add a twist of fancy yarn to the top of her head for hair. • Jan's feet aren't flat so she won't stand but you can add a magnet or pin-back to her back. Poke hole in top of film container. Glue 3" piece of pipe cleaner into hole. Glue head to pipe cleaner. Wrap neck with fibers.

1. Cover film can with Red Liner tape. Adhere fabric.

2. Tuck top fabric into can. Glue the edge inside.

3. Roll fabric around a straw.

4. Insert a pipe cleaner into hole in dice.

5. Insert the end of pipe cleaner into hole in lid.

6. Cover the pipe cleaner with a rolled bead.

7. Twist fibers and wire for doll arms.

8. Glue game pieces onto bottom of lid for legs.

Rolled Bead Dolls

Here's a great project to do with kids. These rolled bead dolls are fun to make with simple materials - glue, straws, fabric scraps, and wire. Design your own faces for a doll that is uniquely yours.

Stamp Face	• easy assembly • teenie beads & sticky tape
Button Face	• easy assembly • used wires & beads
Checker Face	• button feet • wire hair & hands

FINISHED SIZE: 4¹/₂" tall
MATERIALS:
12 strips fabric 1¹/₂" x 1¹/₂" • Drinking straws • *Aleene's* Tacky glue •36" of 22 gauge wire per doll

INSTRUCTIONS:
Make fabric bead: Cut a straw into 1" sections. Dab glue on one end of fabric piece. Roll tightly around straw. Dab glue on end of fabric to secure. • **Doll body:** Glue 6 rolled fabric beads together to form torso and 1 bead across top to form shoulders..

Tip: A rolled fabric bead is a straw covered with fabric.

Button Face Doll

MATERIALS:
4 large glass beads (hands, feet) • Wood stick ¹/₄" x 2" (neck) • Small button, large button (face) • 4 yds yarn for hair • 1 silk ribbon flower

INSTRUCTIONS:
Legs: Cut 22 gauge wire 10" long. Tightly coil one end. Slide on large glass bead for foot. Add fabric bead for leg. Insert wire up into a body bead. Bend wire across top of body. Bring wire down another body bead. Add fabric bead and large glass bead for other foot. Tightly coil wire. • **Neck:** Glue neck stick into center back fabric bead. • **Arms:** Cut 22 gauge wire 6" long. • Tightly coil 1 end. Slide on large glass bead for hand. Place fabric bead over wire. Slide wire through shoulder bead. Slide another fabric bead onto wire. Add large glass bead at end. Make tight coil to secure bead. • Bend arms down beside body. • **Face:** Glue small button on larger button. • Glue to neck stick. • **Hair:** Wind yarn around a 6" piece of cardboard. Slide off end. Knot in middle. Glue to back of head. • Glue silk ribbon flower at neck.

Polka Dot Doll

MATERIALS:
4 Leaf Beads • *Zettiology* face stamp • Tan cardstock • Red Liner tape • Tiny no-hole beads • Fibers

INSTRUCTIONS:
Legs: Cut 22 gauge wire 10" long. Slide on leaf bead for foot. Twist end of wire to secure bead. • Add fabric bead for leg. Insert wire up into a body bead. Bend wire across top of body. Bring wire down another body bead. Add fabric bead and leaf bead for other foot. Tightly coil wire.
Arms: Cut 22 gauge wire 6" long. • Tightly coil 1 end. Slide on leaf bead for hand. Place fabric bead over wire. Slide wire through shoulder bead. Slide another fabric bead onto wire. Add leaf bead at end. Make tight coil to secure bead.
Face: Stamp face on Tan cardstock. Color with pencils. • Cover cardboard with Red liner tape. Add face and fibers.
Neck: Fold 8" wire into fourths. Tape to back of head, leaving 1" stub for neck. • Cover back of head with tape. Cover entire back of head with no-hole beads.
Collar: Cover a 1³/₄" square of tape with no-hole beads on both sides. • Cut hole in center of square. • Place collar on neck. Dip end of neck wire in Tacky glue. Insert through collar and center of shoulder bead.

Checker Face Doll

MATERIALS:
2 Buttons for feet • Checker game piece • Red Liner tape • Copper no-hole beads

INSTRUCTIONS:
Legs: Cut 22 gauge wire 10" long. Tightly coil one end. Slide through hole in button for foot. Add fabric bead for leg. Insert wire up into a body bead. Bend wire across top of body. Bring wire down another body bead. Add fabric bead and button for other foot. Tightly coil wire.
Neck: Insert 2" neck wire through middle of fabric bead for shoulder. Glue end to secure. Glue shoulder bead across top of body with coil hidden. (See photo).
Arms: Cut 22 gauge wire 6" long. • Tightly coil 1 end. Place fabric bead over wire. Pass wire through bead that lays across body beads. Slide another fabric bead onto wire. Make tight coil to secure bead. Bend coils up. • Bend arms down beside body.

HEAD PATTERN

CHECKER HEAD
(drill holes on sides at arrows)

1. Slide head wire through shoulder bead. Twist end.

2. Glue shoulder bead to one end of body.

3. Run wire with leg up through body bead and back down through next bead.

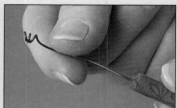

4. Add fabric bead to arm wire.

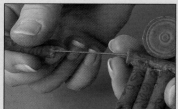

5. Run arm wire through shoulder bead.

6. Remove tape liner from top of head.

7. Wrap top of head with fiber.

8. Attach neck wire with Red liner tape.

9. Cover back of head with Red liner tape and beads.

10. Cut hole in center of collar.

11. Push neck through hole in collar.

Checker Face Doll... continued

Face: Drill holes in checker. See diagram.

Hair: Place tape across head between hair holes. • Coil 18" of 22 gauge wire on pencil. Slide off pencil. Bend at each end. • Dip ends in glue and insert wires into drilled holes. Press wire on tape. Pour Copper no-hole beads on exposed tape. Glue head to neck wire.

Decoration: Wrap fibers around chest. Glue in place.

Domino Dolls

Turn old dominoes into a charming set of dolls. Hang them on the wall, or make a center-piece for family game night.

- dominoes
- wire
- Prismacolor pencils

(She will stand, just fiddle with her legs)

Domino Donna

FINISHED SIZE: 6 1/2" tall

MATERIALS:
Dominoes (4 large, 2 mini) • *Prismacolor* pencils • Teal 22 gauge wire • Popsicle stick • 1 1/2" wooden circle • *Aleene's* Tacky glue • 3 yds fibers for hair • Drill • 1/16" drill bit

INSTRUCTIONS:

Body: Drill small holes in dominoes as shown. • Lay 2 horizontally for body, 2 vertically for legs. Attach dominoes with 2" wires as follows: Bend wire into a "u" shape. Insert 1 end into left hole in upper body and other into left hole in lower body. Pull wire towards back of doll. Twist. Make small coil in back to secure. Cut off excess. • Repeat for right side of body. Add legs and feet.

Arms: Cut two 6" wires. Coil wire around pencil. Slide off end. Insert end of one wire into hole at right shoulder, make small coil to secure. • Repeat for left arm.

ace: Draw face onto wooden circle. • Drill five small holes in wooden circle, 1/8" from edge. (See diagram) • Glue popsicle stick to back of circle, then to back of body. Adjust so you get a neck that is 1/2" long.

Hair: Cut 8" wire. Loop through five holes at top of head. • Cut 15 pieces yarn 6" long. Use 3 pieces for each hair section. Fold yarn in half. Loop through wire. • Repeat for each wire loop.

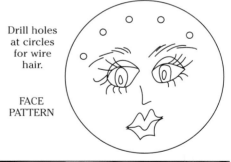

Drill holes at circles for wire hair.

FACE PATTERN

1. Attach hair.

2. Coil arms.

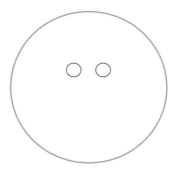

FACE
PATTERN

• red liner tape
• no-hole beads
• dominoes
• colored wire
• metal leaf or Lumiere paint
• Diamond Glaze for clock parts

1. Apply Gold leaf, burnish.

2. Drill holes.

3. Add arm.

4. Add hair and eyes.

5. Pour on no-hole beads.

6. Glue watch parts to body.

Domino Dude

MATERIALS:

1¹/₂" flat button • 2 Black seed beads • 18 gauge wire • Watch parts • 2 dominoes • *JudiKins* Diamond Glaze • *Hero Arts* Criss-Cross Splatter stamp • *StazOn* Black ink pad • Fibers • *Amy's* (Leafing adhesive, Metallic leafing flakes) • Formica sample chip • *Jacquard* Green Lumiere paint • Drill • ¹/₈" drill bit • Red Liner tape • No-hole beads • Magnet

INSTRUCTIONS:

Paint wood side of Formica chip with Lumiere paint. Apply leafing adhesive to formica. Let adhesive set for 15 minutes. Apply metal leafing flakes. Burnish by rubbing with scrap of fabric. • Use Black ink to stamp design on leafed area. • Drill small holes in formica to attach arms and legs.

For each arm: Cut 3" of wire. Coil end of wire. Thread through shoulder hole from front to back. Bend long end of wire down and into an arm shape. Coil end for hand.

For each leg: Drill hole in short end of dominoes. Cut 2" wire. Insert one end through formica, then through domino. Coil on top of formica and behind domino to secure leg.

Face: Cover button with Red Liner tape. Peel liner. Place 2 Black seed beads for eyes. • Cut fibers into 2" long sections for hair. Apply to upper edge of taped head. Pour tiny no-hole beads to cover face. Attach to body using Diamond Glaze.

Finishing: Use Diamond Glaze to attach watch parts or other embellishments to front of body, and to attach magnet to back of doll.

Pretty as a Picture Dolls

Make these dolls in rich tones of fabric and hang them from your Christmas tree. Dress one up for Valentine's Day to decorate a wreath. These easy-to-make dolls adapt readily to any occasion.

FINISHED SIZE: 7" tall
MATERIALS:
Design Originals Slide Mount (#0977 White) or a 1³/₄" wooden disc (for face) • Color photocopy of face • Fabric • Colored wire • Fibers • *Ancient Page* Sage ink pad • Copper brads • 2 hand shaped beads • Leaf beads • 20 size 6 beads • ¹/₄" Copper tape • Heavy duty aluminum foil • ¹/₈" hole punch • *Aleene's* Tacky glue • Heat gun • Pipe cleaners

How to Make the Body

1. Wrap body with batting.

2. Cover body with fabric.

3. Fold over, glue ends of fabric.

BODY PATTERN
(solid line is cutting line for fabric)
(dotted line is cutting line for batting)

INSTRUCTIONS:
Body: Cut 10" square of heavy duty aluminum foil. Fold into flattened cone shape. Use pattern to cut quilt batting and fabric.
Cover foil with light coat of glue and wrap in quilt batting. Trim excess batting off top edge.
Apply line of glue along one straight edge of fabric. Place glued edge on batting. Glue fabric over batting.
Fold top edge of fabric towards back. Glue in place.
Stitch beads on bottom tip of body.

Green-Eyed Girl

INSTRUCTIONS:
Head: Glue color photocopy of face onto a 1³/₄" wooden disc. • Paint back and edges of disc.
Arms: Twist 2 pipe cleaners together. Fold them in half. Apply light layer of glue. • Cut fabric 6" x 1" wide. Center pipe cleaner along one edge of fabric. Fold ends of fabric towards center, and roll fabric around pipe cleaner. Glue to secure edge. • Wrap arms with wire, winding tightly at wrists. Make small coils for hands.
Attach arms: Center arms on back of shoulder area and stitch in place. Bend arms into desired pose. • Glue head to body. Hold in place with clothespin until dry.
Collar: Cut 12" wire. Fold in fourths and twist. Wrap fibers around wire. Tie ends. Place at front of neck and bend ends towards back of head. Stitch in place at back of neck. Glue leaf bead to front of body.

Pretty as a Picture

- slide frame
- Ancient Page inks
- wire
- beads
- wrapped body on aluminum foil & quilt batting base

Pretty as a Picture

INSTRUCTIONS:

Face: Press slide mount onto Sage ink. Set with heat gun. • Insert photo into slide mount. Double-stick tape closed. • Apply Copper tape around edge of slide mount. • Punch holes in upper 2 corners and insert and set Copper brads. • Punch 2 holes in lower edge of slide mount.

Head: Use awl to make 2 holes in upper body 3/4" from top edge and 1" apart. • Cut 5" wire. Fold into "u" shape. Insert wire ends into holes in slide mount, then through holes in doll. Pull wire snug to back and twist ends to secure.

For each arm: Cut 3" wire. • Loop end of wire around the wire that holds the head on. Twist to secure. String on 10 size 6 beads, then a hand bead. Loop wire back through hand bead. Tightly coil wire around the wrist to secure beads. • Attach leaf bead to front of body with wire. Loop it around wire used to attach face.

1. Tint slide mount with an ink pad.

2. Punch holes.

3. Insert wire in holes under face.

Beaded Dolls

Let these beaded beauties add sparkle and color wherever you are... to your window or holiday gifts.

Small Red Doll with Heart

FINISHED SIZE: 3" tall

MATERIALS:
Wire (18 gauge, 26 gauge) • Heart bead • Tan *Premo* polymer clay • *Polyform* face mold

INSTRUCTIONS:
Body is made same way as Yellow Doll.
Dress: Bend 12" wire into doll shape. • Wrap first inch of 26 gauge wire around neck and through arms, where 18 gauge wires all cross. Bring wire to front of neck. • String on 1/2" of seed beads, heart bead, then more seed beads, making length of bead covered wire equal the distance from neck to center hem of dress. • Hold wire against center hem of dress so beads are in a line down center of doll. Hold beads taut and wrap wire twice around frame at center hem of dress. • Add seed beads on wire from hem to neck. • Continue stringing a variety of beads, working in a vertical and/or diagonal pattern until you have filled in dress frame with beads.
Arms: Use same wrapping technique.
Face: Make polymer clay face following manufacturer's directions.• Glue face to neck wires.
Hair: Glue fibers. Cut circle of fabric slightly smaller than back of head. Glue to back of head.

Large Yellow Doll

FINISHED SIZE: 5" tall

MATERIALS:
Wire (18 gauge , 26 gauge) • Beads • Fibers • *Aleene's* Tacky glue • 3 yds *DMC* Flower thread

INSTRUCTIONS:
Dress: Bend 18 gauge wire into doll shape. • Wrap first 3" of 26 gauge wire around neck and through arms, where 18 gauge wires all cross. Bring wire to front of neck. • String on 1/2" of seed beads, three heart shaped beads, then more seed beads, making length of bead covered wire equal the distance from neck to center hem of dress. • Hold wire against center of hem of dress so beads are in a line down center of doll. Hold beads taut and wrap wire twice around frame at center hem of dress. • Continue stringing a variety of beads, working in a vertical and/or diagonal pattern until you have filled in dress frame with beads.
Arms: Use same wrapping technique. Wire size 8 beads at ends of arms to represent hands.
Face: Make a "Sweet Potato" doll face following instructions on page 8-9. • Insert neck wires into back of head. • Cut circle of fabric slightly smaller than back of head. Glue to back of head.
Hair: Wrap flower thread around 4 fingers. Tie in center, then slide off fingers. Glue to back of head.
Finishing: Cut 1 yard of fuzzy yarn. Tie around neck. Wind in "x" pattern to cover exposed neck wires. Tie off ends in back of doll.

BITTY RED DOLL PATTERN

LARGE YELLOW DOLL PATTERN

How to Make the Red and Yellow Beaded Doll Bodies

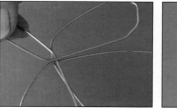  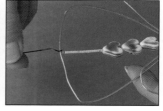 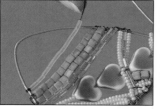

1. Shape wire body.

2. Wire together at neck.

3. Wrap beaded wire to center of dress.

4. Wrap beaded wires around frame.

How to Make Bitty Buddies Doll Body

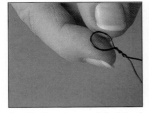

1. Twist top of folded wire to form loop.

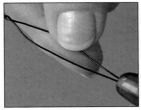

2. Insert both ends of wire into large bead.

3. For arms, twist wire around neck.

Pony Tail Red Bitty Doll

INSTRUCTIONS:

Face and fiber hair: Glue face to head loop. Glue hair to back of face. Add more glue, and a small piece of felt to cover fiber ends.

Green and Purple Bitty Doll

INSTRUCTIONS:

Face and fiber hair: Glue face to head loop. Glue leaf bead to back of head. • Embellish doll with fibers.

Bitty Beaded Buddies

Use the small dolls as jewelry and trinkets.

FINISHED SIZE: 3" tall

MATERIALS:
22 gauge wire • Beads • *Aleene's* Tacky glue • Tan *Premo* polymer clay • *Polyform* face mold • Cornstarch • Fibers • Gold *Metallic Rub Ons* • E-6000 • Pin back • Large leaf bead • Felt scrap

INSTRUCTIONS:
Body: Fold 8" wire in half. Twist top to form a 1/2" loop. • Insert both ends of wire into large bead. Place 1" of beads on each wire. Tightly coil each end. Bend to form foot.
Arms: Wrap middle of 5" wire around neck twice. Add beads for arms. Tightly coil ends.
Head: Make polymer clay face following manufacturer's directions.

Collage Dolls

These dolls would make a wonderful gift for a little girl. Collage the bodies with Victorian underwear. Make templates for clothes, and create your very own set of paper dolls.

FINISHED SIZE: 7" tall

MATERIALS:
Wooden doll shape (or cut your own from cardboard) • Skin tone acrylic paints • *Golden* Regular Gel Medium • Decorative papers • Face images or photos • *Ancient Page* Sienna ink • Stipple brush • *Aleene's* Tacky glue • Ephemera • Lace • Buttons • Metallic thread

INSTRUCTIONS:
Use either purchased wooden doll shapes or cut your own out of cardboard. • Paint doll. Let dry. • Use gel medium to layer papers onto doll shapes. Use sheet music, old letters, paper napkins, photocopies of photographs, and scraps of fancy papers. Remove air bubbles by pushing them out with fingertip. • Cut faces out of photographs or Victorian reproduction wrapping paper. Glue to doll using gel medium. • To give doll "antique" look, stipple with Sienna inks. Glue bits of lace and old buttons. • Wrap thin metallic threads around doll.

To make hanging doll, cut a 2" x 1" piece of cardstock, fold in half. Punch hole in end of cardstock. Glue folded end to back of doll. Insert hook into hole to hang.

1. Paint wood.

2. Glue papers.

3. Stipple or age.

4. Add details.

Collage on wood

- collage
- stipple with inks to antique
- wrapped with wire and/or tinsel

DOLL PATTERN

Jointed Dolls

Make interesting doll dresses with beading and embossing techniques. Cut magazine images for faces, or use a family photo. These dolls have moveable arms and legs assembled with brads.

GENERAL MATERIALS:
Design Originals Slide Mount (#0977 White) • Lightweight cardboard • Red Liner tape • Tiny no-hole beads • *StazOn* Black ink • *Tsukineko* (All Purpose Ink, Fantastix applicator) • Brads • Decorative paper • Prismacolor pencils • *Character Constructions* E-006 rubber stamp • *Aleene's* Tacky glue • 1/8" hole punch • Craft knife • 6" wire 24 gauge • Magnet • Clear embossing powder • Face image

Bella Doll
Uses red liner tape & several layers of embossing powder to make the body more solid and sturdy

Bella Doll

FINISHED SIZE: 8 1/2" tall
INSTRUCTIONS:
Body: Rubber stamp body parts onto cardstock.
Dress: Glue decorative paper to cardboard. Trace dress pattern on back. Cut out. Cover front with Red liner tape. Peel away top layer of tape and apply clear embossing powder. Melt powder with heat tool. Apply at least four layers of melted embossing powder.
Head: Cut out picture of face with neck. Glue to popsicle stick. Glue stick to back of doll. Attach arms and legs to dress with brads.

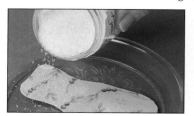

1. Cover body with clear embossing powder..

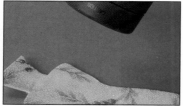

2. Heat.

Beaded Beauty
• uses slide frame • brads
• red liner tape • no-hole beads

Beaded Beauty

FINISHED SIZE: 9" tall
INSTRUCTIONS:
Body: Rubber stamp body parts onto cardstock.
Dress: Glue decorative paper to cardboard. Trace dress pattern on back. Cut out. Cover front with Red liner tape. Peel tape. Cover with no-hole beads. • Punch holes in top of arms and legs. Punch holes in dress at shoulders and hem. Attach arms and legs with brads.
Head: Cover front of slide mount with tape. Use craft knife to cut out center hole. • Glue image inside slide mount. Peel away top layer of tape. Cover with no-hole beads.
Attach Head: Fold wire in fourths. Tape one end to back of head, other end to back of body. • Glue a magnet to the back of head.

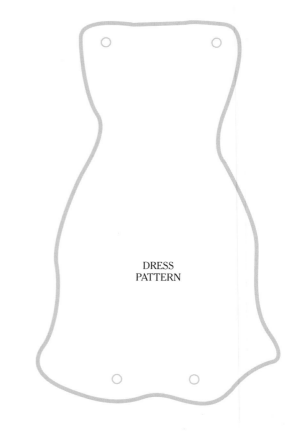

DRESS PATTERN

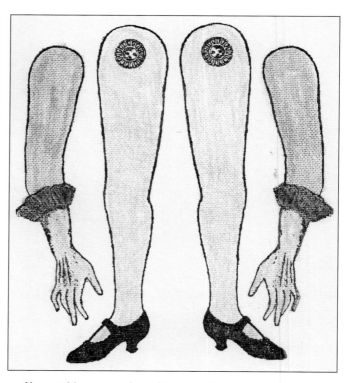

Use a rubber stamp from Character Constructions to make the arms and legs. Color with pencils, markers or chalk if desired. Cut out the arms and legs, punch a hole and attach to the body with small brads or eyelets.

1. Gather skirt with Running stitch.

2. Gather skirt to fit paint stick.

3. Glue head to top of paint stick.

4. Drill holes for legs.

5. Attach legs with brads.

6. Embellish doll.

Paint Stick Chicks

Generate some chatter when you make these dolls with the faces of your friends. Stand them up in a flower centerpiece at your next party. Write their names on the stick, and new friends will identify everyone more easily.

Paint Stick Chicks

- re-inkers
- stamps
- red liner tape

Wouldn't it be a great swap? Each person could make one of themself, then swap so you have a whole collection of "friends".

FINISHED SIZE: 11" to 11 1/2" tall

MATERIALS:
Paint stick • *Character Constructions* E-006 arms/legs stamp • *StazOn* ink pad (Black, Gold) • Fabric • Fibers • *Aleene's* Tacky Glue • Wire • Brads • Red Liner tape • No-hole beads • Acrylic Paint • 1/8" hole punch

INSTRUCTIONS:
Paint the stick:: Paint the wood stick with desired color acrylic paint. Stamp designs on stick with *StazOn* ink.

Skirt:: Cut fabric 5" x 2 1/2". Overlap back seam. Glue closed. Make Running stitch around top edge of skirt. Slip over paint stick and pull thread snug. Stitch to secure gathers. Reach under skirt and add a few dabs of glue at waist to secure.

Dress: Cut cardstock bodice. Cover bodice with no-hole beads if desired. Glue to paint stick, tucking lower edge of bodice into waist of skirt. • Wrap fibers or ribbon around waist for a belt.

Face: Cut face out of photocopy. Glue to cardstock to stiffen. • Tuck neck into blouse. Glue to stick.

Arms/Legs: Stamp arms and legs on cardstock. Color, cut out, and punch hole at top. • Drill small holes in stick where arm and leg holes line up. Attach arms and legs to stick with brads. Embellish doll using beads, wire, buttons, bits of lace, or decorative fibers.

DRESS
TOP
PATTERN
FOR
BLOUSE

Bingo-lina

Decorate your door and let Bingo-lina greet your guests for a Bingo party. This sturdy, 16" doll also makes a nice wall hanging.

Easy assembly with eyelets, wire, glue
- Lumiere paints
- red liner tape
- embossing powder
- eyelets
- wire
- rubber stamping
- Prismacolor pencils

FINISHED SIZE: 16" tall

MATERIALS:
2 Bingo cards • Bingo game pieces • 2 paint sticks • 6" Red 22-24 gauge wire • 4 wooden ice cream spoons • *Jacquard* Super Copper Lumiere paint • Red Liner tape • Clear embossing powder • Clear embossing ink • UTEE • Small eyelets • Rubber stamps (*Postmodern Designs* Hands Cube; *Stamp In the Hand* face #Q-1940; *Hero Arts* Tiny Stars, Numbers) • *Prismacolor* pencils • Tan cardstock • Decorative paper • Lightweight cardboard • *Aleene's* Tacky glue • *StazOn* Black ink pad • 1/8" hole punch

INSTRUCTIONS:

Arms, Legs, Skirt: Paint both sides of 2 paint sticks, 4 spoons, and back of Bingo card with Copper. Let dry. • Rubber stamp designs on paint sticks and spoons with Black ink. • Drill small holes into both ends of spoons. • Cut decorative paper 4" x 15" for skirt. Fold paper into pleats so pleated skirt is same width as bottom of Bingo card. • Place a 1" wide strip of Red Liner tape on lower back edge of Bingo card. Tape front of skirt to back of card, leaving sides for skirt back loose. Glue front pleats in place. • Trim skirt to desired length.

Feet: Cut a row of 5 Bingo numbers from Bingo card. Fold over two number squares. • Glue numbers to end of paint sticks, placing three numbers in the front, two in back. Glue wooden Bingo number on top edge of shoe. For legs, glue paint sticks to back of Bingo card. Glue pleats and back skirt seam.

Body: Punch holes in top corners of Bingo card. Set eyelets. •

Hands: Stamp hands on Tan cardstock. Color with pencils. • Punch 1/8" hole at wrist. Emboss several layers for a thick and even coat.

Body Assembly: Cut 6 wires 1" long. • Place wide end of 1 spoon behind right shoulder hole on Bingo card. Insert a wire through shoulder and spoon. Twirl tight coil in front of shoulder and behind spoon. • Attach lower arm and hand using the same method. • Repeat for left arm. • Pose arms and glue in place if desired.

Face: Stamp face with Black on Tan cardstock. Color with pencils. Cut out. • Cut cardboard circle slightly smaller than stamped image. Glue cardstock onto cardboard circle for added strength. Paint back of cardboard circle with Copper paint. • Punch 1/8" hole at lower edge of head. Set eyelet. • Attach head to body using wire. • Glue Bingo numbers and markers as shown.

1. Paint and stamp paint sticks.

2. Gather skirt onto Bingo card.

3. Glue legs to back of Bingo card.

4. Fold skirt over legs. Glue in place.

5. Stamp and color face.

Whimsical Create Doll

Meal preparation is an art. Hang this spoon doll in your kitchen to inspire your creativity.

- torn paper for body
- stamped & embossed

Products:
- eyelets
- beads
- colored wire
- wire hands
- grommet letters
- Gel Medium
- rubber stamp
- wire mesh

1. Attach arms to body.

2. Position spoon on back of dress.

3. Use arm wire to hold the spoon in place.

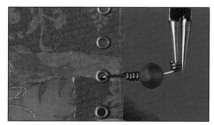

4. Coil fringe wire.

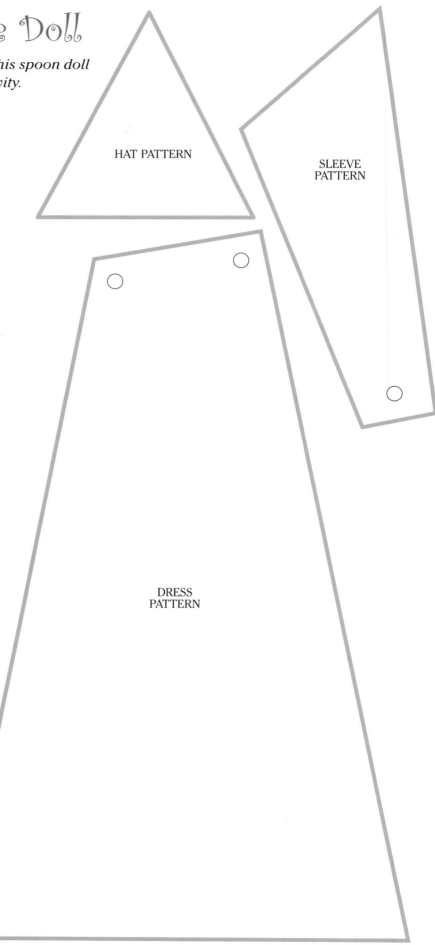

HAT PATTERN

SLEEVE PATTERN

DRESS PATTERN

FINISHED SIZE: 16" tall

MATERIALS:
Wooden spoon • Fibers for hair • Decorative papers • Copper wire (12" of 18 gauge, 27" of 22 gauge) • Wire hands • *Krylon* metallic pen • 19 eyelets, long • *Making Memories* Letter eyelets • Glass beads • Acrylic paint • *Prismacolor* pencils • Rubber stamps (*Magenta* Dragonfly; *Postmodern Design* Compassion) • *StazOn* Black ink • *Encore* Champagne ink pad • 8" ribbon ¹/₄" wide • Light-weight cardboard • *Golden* Regular Gel Medium • ¹/₈" hole punch • Eyelet tools • *AMACO* WireMesh Copper woven fabric

INSTRUCTIONS:

Body: Paint wooden spoon with acrylic paint. • Use gel medium to collage strips of decorative papers to cardboard. Let dry. • Stamp dragonfly with Champagne ink. • Cut dress and arms out of collage cardboard. Apply *Krylon* metallic ink around edges of dress parts. • Punch 2 holes at shoulder to attach arms, 1 hole at top and wrist of each arm, and a row of holes along bottom edge of dress.

For each arm: Attach to body by inserting long eyelet into dress, then through arm. Set eyelets. • Use long eyelets to attach hands at wrists.

Dress: Set 9 eyelets in holes on dress bottom. • To add beads, cut 9 pieces of 22 gauge wire 3" long. Tightly coil end. Add bead. Insert end of wire into hole. Fold wire over. Wrap end of wire around wire near bead. Repeat for all holes in hem. • Punch 6 holes down center of dress. Set eyelet letters.

Face: Stamp face on back of wooden spoon with Black ink. Color with pencils.

Attach dress to spoon handle, cut 18 gauge wire 6" long. Coil 1 end. Insert into eyelet at shoulder. Wrap wire around spoon. Bring end of wire out of other shoulder. Tightly coil to secure.

Finish: Cut 8" of ¹/₄" wide ribbon. Tie bow around neck. • Glue hair fibers to back of spoon. • For hat, cover triangle with wire mesh. Wrap hat with 18 gauge wire. Add bead at tip of hat. Glue to head.

Tips for Drawing the Face

Eyes are about halfway down the face.

Use a Brown pen to draw features.

Add touches of Black to eyebrows and eyelashes only. Use a light touch and go over the lines several times until satisfied with results.

Black pupil and White highlight in eyes give the eyes "life". Place pupils so doll is looking a little down and left. Placing pupils center creates a staring lifeless expression.

This is a cartoon face, don't worry if the eyes aren't exactly the same or if the nose is a little crooked. It isn't supposed to look like a real person.

Wild Woman

She's a little sassy, a little brassy - that secret "wild" we keep inside. Set her free by making one of these fun dolls. Nobody has to know she is your alter ego!

FINISHED SIZE: 14" tall

MATERIALS:

Fabric • Fibers • Chopsticks • Old thread spools • 22 gauge wire • Hand beads • Silamide or Nymo beading thread • Beading needle • *Pigma* Micron .005 pens (Black, Brown, Green, Red) • Old jewelry for embellishing • *Poly-fil* stuffing • Crystal glitter • Tracing paper • Drinking straws • *Aleene's* Tacky glue • *Prismacolor* pencils

INSTRUCTIONS:

Body: Place fabric right sides together. Trace pattern on fabric. • Sew on traced line. Leave 2" opening at bottom. • Cut out, leaving 1/4" seam allowance. Clip curves, turn right sides out. Stuff doll body tightly. Stitch opening closed.

egs: Use fancy chopsticks or paint plain ones with Tan paint and draw designs with fine point marker.

Feet: Dip end of chopstick into glue. Insert into spool. Let dry. • Poke holes in bottom edge of body. Dip top end of chopstick into glue and insert into body. Repeat for other leg.

Arms: Tear fabric into 1 1/2" by 2" pieces. Cut drinking straw into 1 1/4" long sections. Put a dab of glue on end of fabric. Roll fabric around straw, secure end with dab of glue. Make 4. • For each arm, cut 6" of 22 gauge wire. Poke hole through fabric at shoulder. Insert wire and twist to secure. Add 2 fabric beads to wire. Tightly coil at wrist end. Bend at elbow. • Sew hand bead to end of arm and stitch hand to hip to hold pose.

Face: Use Brown markers to draw face in center of 2 1/4" circle of muslin. Cut out muslin circle. See Tips for Drawing Faces.

Fabric: Cut a 2" circle of quilt batting, and a 1 1/2" circle of cardboard. • Layer muslin over batting and center both on cardboard circle. • Make Running stitches around edge of muslin, just inside raw edge. Pull thread snug, so muslin and batting are drawn tightly around edge of cardboard circle. Make a few stitches in back to secure thread end. • When face is finished apply light layer of crystal glitter.

Bead around the face with a Picot Stitch:

Attach body: Sew doll face to neck stub on doll body.

Decorate: Wrap ribbon around neck. Tie into bow with long tails. • Glue fibers to back of head for hair. • Breasts are old flower-shaped earrings, glued to doll with Tacky glue.

How to Make a Picot Stitch

Picot Stitch: Thread beading needle with beading thread. Make a few stitches in back of head to secure and bring needle out in the edge. Put 3 seed beads on needle and go down through edge. Bring thread back out bead through #3. Add 2 beads to needle. Go through edge to secure. Continue around face to beginning.

Lacy Picot Stitch: Bring thread out through beads #1 & #2. Add 4 beads. Go down through beads #6 & #7 into edge. Come back out through beads #5 & #6. Add 4 beads. Go down through beads #10 & #11 into edge. Bring thread out through beads #9 & #10. Continue around face to beginning. Knot thread on back.

BODY
PATTERN
Cut 2
Add a 1/4"
seam allowance

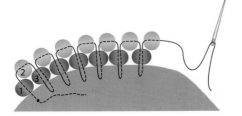
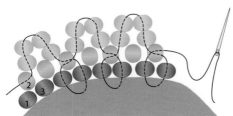

"Tin Woman"
- Altoids tin case
- Diamond Glaze
- Lumiere paints
- wrapped arms with pipe cleaner and fibers

Tin Woman

Here's a two-sided project that could be used in a centerpiece or gift basket. An accordion fold card holds a special message inside.

FINISHED SIZE: 7" tall

MATERIALS:

Altoid tin for body • 2 thimbles • Watch parts tin for head• 6" of 22 gauge wire • 4 yds fibers • 60" yarn for hair • Color images • Green *Jacquard* Lumiere paint • *Golden* Regular Gel Medium • *JudiKins* Diamond Glaze • Beads • Old jewelry • 1/8" hole punch • Sandpaper • Tapestry fabric scrap • Decorative paper scraps • Pipe cleaners • Small nail • 3" x 15" cardstock • 2 long brads

INSTRUCTIONS:

Body: Punch holes in body tin: 2 in shoulder area for arms, 1 for neck, 2 in bottom for legs. • Lightly sand entire tin. • Dab 2 coats paint inside and out using small sponge. Let dry. • Attach image to front and tapestry fabric to back of tin with Gel Medium.

ach arm: Cut 6" pipe cleaner. Fold in half. Wrap pipe cleaner with 2 yards fibers, shaping arms by overlapping yarn where arm is thicker. Leave 1" of pipe cleaner exposed at top of arm. • Insert exposed end of pipe cleaner into hole at shoulder. Coil to secure.

Each leg: Slightly flatten thimble. • Punch a hole in end with a nail. • Paint thimble. • Insert a long brad into thimble, and the hole in tin. Open tabs on brad. Flatten to secure.

Head: Make 1 neck hole in lower edge and five hair holes along upper edge of round tin. • Paint. • Glue face image inside and to back of tin using Diamond Glaze.

Neck: Cut 6" of wire. Coil wire around pencil. Insert 1 end of wire into hole in body tin. Coil end to secure. • Insert other end of neck wire into hole at bottom of head. Coil wire to secure.

Hair: Cut 10 pieces of yarn 6" long. • Loop two pieces of yarn folded in half into each hair hole.

Embellishments: Attach items inside and outside box with Diamond Glaze.

Accordion book inside tin: Draw line 1 1/2" from end of cardstock. This part will glue to tin. • Decorate both sides of cardstock. • Accordion fold cardstock into 1 1/2" sections. • Glue to inside of tin with Diamond Glaze.

1. Punch holes.

2. Wrap arms.

3. Attach hair fibers.

Serenity Art Doll

This elegant doll gets her serene appearance from the face image and soft subtle colors in her gown. Make this collector's prize for yourself or as a gift.

"Serenity"

- almost no sewing
- arms of pipe cleaners, florist tape & Lumiere paint
- easy wrapping, tucking, gluing assembly

FINISHED SIZE: 11" tall

MATERIALS:

1" x 36" fabric (bodice) • 7" x 16" fabric (underskirt and overskirt) • 2" x 4" fabric for belt • Photocopy of face • Fibers • Florist's tape • Silk flowers • 1½" grapevine wreath • Jewelry piece • Two 7" cardboard cones • Green *Jacquard* Lumiere paint • 20 gauge wire • Pipe cleaners • *Aleene's* Tacky glue • *Hearty* clay • *JudiKins* Diamond Glaze • Wooden ice cream spoon • 1½" cardboard circle • Two 1" pom poms • ⅛" Red Liner tape

INSTRUCTIONS:

Cones: • Cut 3" from bottom edge of one cone, then cut 1" from top edge. Do not cut the other cone. Paint both cones with Lumiere paint. • Flatten both cones slightly. • Whole cone is for body. Large cut section is for bodice.

Arms: Twist 2 pipe cleaners together, then fold in thirds. • Wrap pipe cleaners with layers of florist tape, making wider where arms are thicker. • Cut 3" of 20 gauge wire. Fold in half. Place at top of arm, leaving an exposed loop. Secure to arm with florist tape. • Paint arms with Lumiere paint. • Hook arms over edge of bodice cone. • Roll ¼ cup Hearty Clay into an oblong ball. Insert clay into top of bodice, forming shoulders with the clay over arm wires.

Face: Paint wooden ice cream spoon with Lumiere paint. • Glue face to cardboard circle. Glue to painted spoon. Spoon handle is neck.

Bodice: Insert 1" of neck spoon into Hearty Clay. Let dry. Paint clay with Lumiere. • Glue two 1" pom poms to chest for breasts. • Wrap the 1" fabric strip in criss-cross manner around bodice and under arms, smooth out wrinkles. Secure ends of fabric with glue.

Attach Body: Put a silver dollar sized amount of glue inside the narrow end of bodice cone. Place bodice cone on top of pointed end of body cone. • Insert paper towel inside tip of body cone to catch dripping glue. Let dry.

Dress: Hem raw edges of skirts with Red liner tape. Cut tape same length as fabric edge, remove backing, adhere to fabric. Remove liner, fold fabric over once to form hem. Rub fingernail along fabric to secure hem. • Use Running stitch to gather underskirt at waist. • Wrap around waist, draw thread snug and secure thread. • Repeat for overskirt. • Fold raw edges of belt to center. Wrap around waist, stitch or glue at back to secure.

Hair: Glue twisted yarns around neck and back of head.

Finishing: Glue flower bouquet to grapevine wreath. Glue wreath to hands. • Glue jewelry embellishment at neck.

1. Cut cone.

2. Attach arm wire with florist tape.

3. Put clay in bodice cone.

4. Insert spoon into clay.

5. Wrap bodice with fabric strip.

6. Glue bodice cone to skirt cone.

7. Twist fibers for hair. Glue to head.

8. Wrap belt around waist.

Sunshine Doll

Here's a fun way for sunflower lovers to display family photos. Make a whole garden of your family to hang on the wall. This doll can be made two-sided and placed in the center of a plant for a party centerpiece. If you are looking for a smaller project, just make the flower faces.

FINISHED SIZE: 20" tall

MATERIALS:
Eighteen 6" squares and one 10" circle assorted Yellow and Gold fabric • 1/2 yd Dark Green fabric • Two 20" squares canvas fabric • Four 20" squares quilt batting • Eyelets • 2 yds *DMC* Copper floss • Seed beads • *Making Memories* alphabet charms • *JudiKins* (Diamond Glaze, Black Roxs) • 1 1/2" wide wire-edged silk ribbon • 12 yds fibers • Tissue paper (Dark Green, Light Green) • *Brilliance* Copper stamp pad • *Hero Arts* leaf stamp • 2 1/2" *Dritz* half ball cover button • Color photocopy of face • *Golden* Regular Gel Medium • Wire clothes hanger • Pipe cleaner • *Aleene's* Tacky glue • Green *Jacquard* Lumiere paint • 1 yd wire • Hot glue • 24 Binder clips • 1/8" hole punch • Hand shaped charms

INSTRUCTIONS:
Petals around face: Cut eighteen 6" squares Yellow and Gold fabric.
Petal: See Petal diagram. Fold square diagonally. Fold point C to point A and point B to point A. With fingertips, gather across line D. Secure gathers with 6" piece of wire. • Make 18 petals. • Sew one seed bead at tip of each petal to secure fabric layers. • Trim excess fabric 1/2" below wire. • Use hot glue to attach petals to the back of a 2 1/2" cover button.
Face: Cut face image into 2 1/2" circle. Snip edges of photo, 1/4" deep, 1/4" apart, all around photo. This will smooth edges of paper over round edge of button piece. • Apply gel medium to back of image. Place in center of button. Use fingers to work out wrinkles and air bubbles. Let dry.
Ribbon center: Cut a 16" long piece of wire-edged ribbon. Fold ribbon in half lengthwise. Carefully pull wires in both edges to gather ribbon. Adjust length and gathers to fit around the face photo. • Fold under raw ends of ribbon and attach around edge of photo using hot glue. • Apply a line of Diamond Glaze around face, touching ribbon. Let it sit for ten minutes. Pour on Black Roxs. Let dry overnight.

Body Frame: Bend wire hanger into large leaf shape. Cut hanger hook off just above twisted wire section. Discard hook. • Lay hanger diagonally on two pieces of batting, leaving twisted wire (neck) sticking out at corner. Hot glue hanger to batting. Run a bead of hot glue on top of hanger. Lay remaining two pieces of batting on top of hanger. You will have a sandwich of batting with the hanger in the middle. • Carefully trim excess batting away from outer edge, leaving a scant 1/4" of batting all around.

INSTRUCTIONS:

Body Covering: Cut two 20" squares of canvas fabric. Lay body frame diagonally on 2 canvas layers. Leave wire neck sticking out of corner. Trace around body shape, adding 1" all around. • Cut out canvas body layers. Layer canvas, body, canvas. Tacky glue canvas layers to one another, making a flat flange around entire edge. Use paper clips or binder clips to hold edges together until glue dries. • Trim edges to 1/2" flange all around body. • Paint front, back and raw edges with Lumiere paint. Let dry. • Punch holes in flange 1" apart. Set eyelets in each hole. • Cut 5 feet floss. Begin at top right eyelet and wind the floss through all eyelets, overlapping edge of flange. Tie floss ends in front of neck to secure. Leave floss ends long to hang down front of body.

Body Decorations: Cut 6 fibers 2 yds long. Fold in half twice to make 18" long bundle of fibers. Twist to form rope. Wrap with wire to secure. Bend gentle curves into rope and glue to body using hot glue. • Stamp 4 Light Green and 4 Dark Green leaves onto tissue paper with Copper ink. Glue to front of doll using gel medium. • Attach alphabet charms to body using small drops of Diamond Glaze. Let dry overnight.

Arms: Cut two 18" squares of Dark Green fabric. • Fold into leaf shapes like yellow petals. • Before securing gathers with wire, insert pipe cleaner into folded section so you can pose arm. Sew hand to sleeve and stitch arm to body at shoulder. • Pose arms and glue hands to body with Diamond Glaze to hold pose.

Head: Insert twisted wire from hanger through shank on back of button form. Secure by twisting pipe cleaner through loop and around wire. • Stitch through petals and shoulders to hold in place.

Hanger: Insert pipe cleaner into button shank. Twist ends together to form loop. • Cut 10" circle of fabric. Make Running stitches along edge. Draw thread taut. Fabric will pull together to form circle. • Glue to back of head and shoulder area to cover raw edges of fabric. • Leave pipe cleaner loop sticking out at top for hanging.

continued on pages 40 - 41

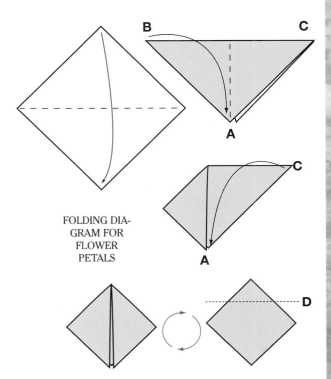

FOLDING DIA-
GRAM FOR
FLOWER
PETALS

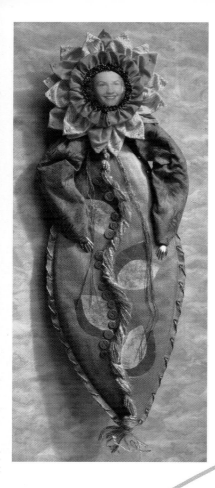

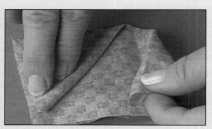

1. Fold a fabric square into a triangle shape.

2. Fold points to the center.

Sunshine Doll... *continued from pages 38 - 39*

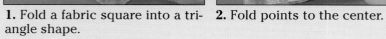

BODY PATTERN
Cut 2
Add a $^1/4$"
seam allowance

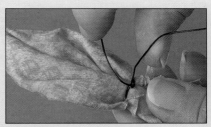

3. Wrap with wire.

4. Glue petals to face button.

"Sunshine"

• no sewing except for beads at tips of petals

Products:

• Lumiere paint
• Gel Medium
• grommets
• metal letters
• Diamond Glaze
• Roxs

Looks complex, but is simple construction. Great for both beginners & experienced doll makers.

BODy PATTERN
Cut 2
Add a ¹/₄"
seam allowance

All Tied Up Girl

Old neckties are great for making dolls since most of the sewing is already done for you. You can raid someone's tie collection or find neckties at thrift shops.

Tips for Drawing the Face

Eyes are about halfway down the face.

Use a Brown pen to draw features.

Add touches of Black to eyebrows and eyelashes only. Use a light touch and go over the lines several times until satisfied with results.

Black pupil and White highlight in eyes give the eyes "life". Place pupils so doll is looking a little down and left. Placing pupils center creates a staring lifeless expression.

This is a cartoon face, don't worry if the eyes aren't exactly the same or if the nose is a little crooked. It isn't supposed to look like a real person.

FACE
PATTERN

How to Make a Picot Stitch

Picot Stitch: Thread beading needle with beading thread. Make a few stitches in back of head to secure and bring needle out in the edge. Put 3 seed beads on needle and go down through edge. Bring thread back out bead through #3. Add 2 beads to needle. Go through edge to secure. Continue around face to beginning.

Lacy Picot Stitch: Bring thread out through beads #1 & #2. Add 4 beads. Go down through beads #6 & #7 into edge. Come back out through beads #5 & #6. Add 4 beads. Go down through beads #10 & #11 into edge. Bring thread out through beads #9 & #10. Continue around face to beginning. Knot thread on back.

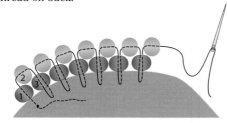

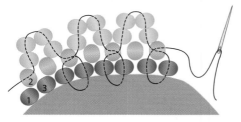

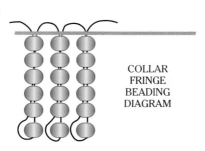

COLLAR
FRINGE
BEADING
DIAGRAM

COUCHING DIAGRAM
(on skirt)

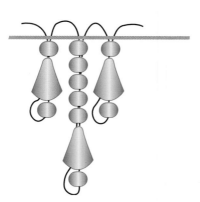

SKIRT FRINGE
BEADING DIAGRAM

FINISHED SIZE: 8" tall

MATERIALS:
Muslin or Flesh tone fabric for body • Sewing supplies • Disappearing fabric marker • *Poly-fil* stuffing • 4 pipe cleaners • Stuffing fork or chopstick • 2 wood beads 3/8" • Beaded fringe • Seed beads • Curly fibers • 2 wide neckties • *Pigma* Micron .005 pens (Brown, Black)

INSTRUCTIONS:

Body: Trace body pattern on doubled piece of muslin or flesh tone fabric. • Sew on traced lines, leaving opening at neck for turning. • Cut out, leaving 1/4" seam allowance. Clip curves. • Turn right side out. Stuff tightly. Stitch neck opening closed.

Legs: Trace leg pattern on doubled muslin or flesh tone fabric. • Sew on traced lines, leaving opening at top for turning. • Cut out, leaving 1/4" seam allowance. Clip curves. • Turn right side out. • Make 2. • Insert pipe cleaner into each fabric leg working fabric over bend in ankle and pushing pipe cleaner all the way to end of fabric foot. Use a stuffing fork or chopstick to stuff legs with poly-fil. Leave legs open at top.

Attach legs: Cut 2 small slits in body to insert pipe cleaners from legs. Adjust legs so they are firmly supporting body. Hand stitch top of legs to bottom of body.

Arms: Fold 1 pipe cleaner in half for each arm. Slide small wooden bead on pipe cleaner. Push bead up to fold to form hand. • Fold over top 1" of pipe cleaner to form a loop to sew through to attach arms to body. Sew arms to body at shoulders.

Dress: Starting from point of tie, cut 8" length from wide end of necktie. • Remove back seam in tie and remove wool lining. Leave silk lining in place. Press out creases. Measure from point of tie, fold down 2" to form triangle on dress bodice, press. Bead fringe along edge of pointed section. Fold under 1/4" on hemline. Stitch in place. Sew beaded fringe trim to hem and add row of beads 1/4" above hem. • Place dress around doll firmly under armpits. Adjust to fit snugly. Sew back of dress.

Sleeves: Measure 5" from point on skinny end of ties, cut two sections for sleeves. Remove back seam stitching and wool lining. Press out creases. For each sleeve, place tie fabric right sides together, sew sleeve seam. Slide sleeve on arm, point end towards neck. Tack in place. Turn right side out. Fold under raw edge around wrist. Hand hem and gather sleeve. Repeat for second arm.

Face: Cut a 2 1/2" circle of muslin, a 1 3/4" circle of quilt batting, and a 1 1/4" circle of cardboard. Layer muslin over batting and center both on cardboard circle. • Make Running stitches around edge of muslin. Pull thread snug, so muslin and batting are drawn tightly around edge of circle. • Make several stitches across back of circle.

Drawing face: See tips for drawing faces. Use Brown pen to draw face. Add touches of Black to eyebrows and eyelashes. • Draw Black pupil and White highlight in eyes to give eyes "life". Place pupils so the doll is looking down and left.

Assembly: Stitch head to neck. Glue curly fibers to back of head for hair. • Adjust pose.

body patterns continued on pages 44 - 45

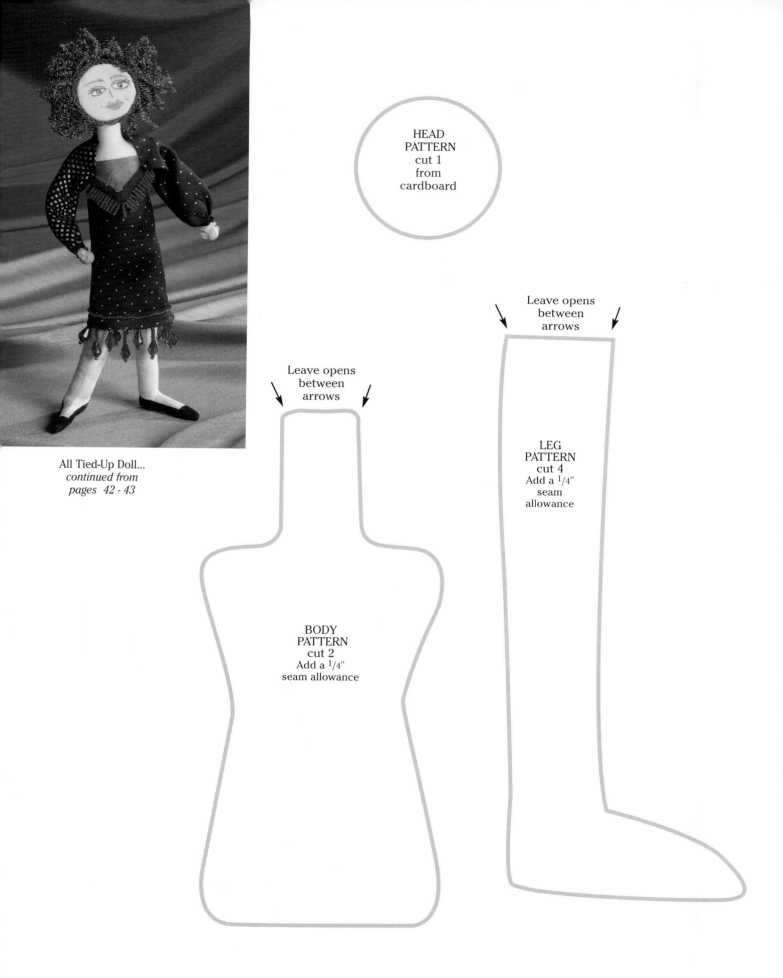

HEAD
PATTERN
cut 1
from
cardboard

All Tied-Up Doll...
*continued from
pages 42 - 43*

Leave opens
between
arrows

Leave opens
between
arrows

LEG
PATTERN
cut 4
Add a $1/4$"
seam
allowance

BODY
PATTERN
cut 2
Add a $1/4$"
seam allowance

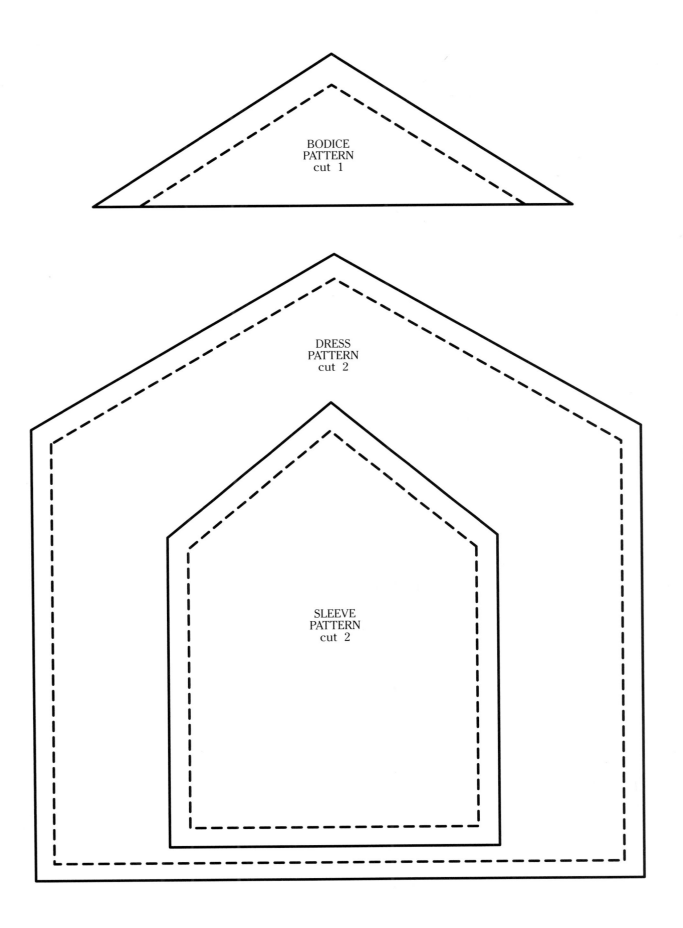

BODICE
PATTERN
cut 1

DRESS
PATTERN
cut 2

SLEEVE
PATTERN
cut 2

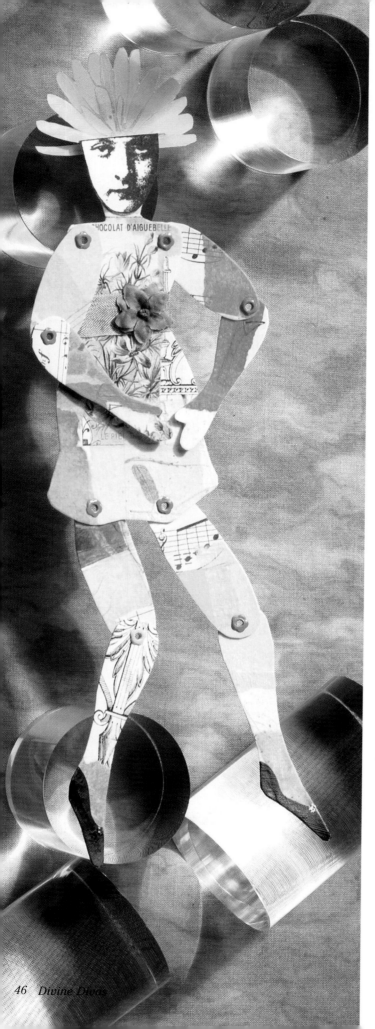

Flower Girl

FINISHED SIZE: 8" tall

GENERAL MATERIALS:
Posterboard • *Golden* Regular Gel Medium • Brads or flower shaped eyelets • Assorted decorative papers • *Zettiology* face rubber stamp • Black dye based ink pad • Black permanent marker • *Stickles* glitter glue • Embellishments • Foam brush • 1/8" hole punch

INSTRUCTIONS:

Collage: Tear decorative papers into random shapes. Randomly glue torn papers onto posterboard using gel medium applied with a foam brush. Let dry. • Trace pattern pieces onto collage. Cut out. • Punch 1/8" holes where indicated on pattern.

Assemble body with flower shaped eyelets. • Use Black marker to draw shoes. Embellish shoes with a drop of Stickles glitter glue. •

Dress: Glue ribbon and silk flower at waist.

Face: Stamp face onto White cardstock. Cut out. Glue over face area on body pattern. • From flower-designed paper, cut out flower for hat. Cut slit in flower. Place on head. Glue in place.

Grommet Doll

• make a large collage sheet, then cut out parts for several dolls
• use Gel Medium for collage sheet

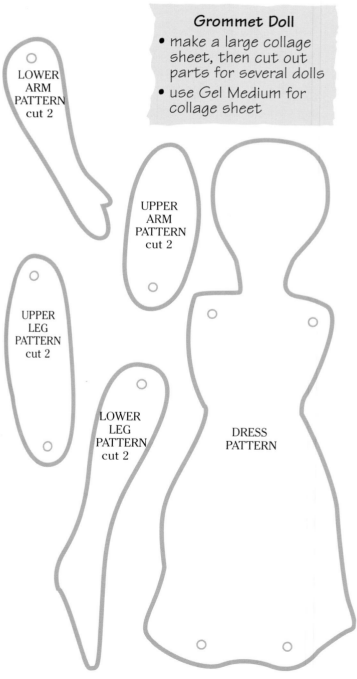

LOWER ARM PATTERN cut 2

UPPER ARM PATTERN cut 2

UPPER LEG PATTERN cut 2

LOWER LEG PATTERN cut 2

DRESS PATTERN

FINISHED SIZE: 5 1/2" tall

GENERAL MATERIALS:

Posterboard • *Golden* Regular Gel Medium • Brads or flower shaped eyelets • Assorted decorative papers • *Zettiology* face rubber stamp • Black dye based stamp pad • Black permanent marker • *Stickles* glitter glue • Embellishments • Foam brush • 1/8" hole punch • Red Liner tape • No-hole beads

INSTRUCTIONS:

Collage: Tear decorative papers into random shapes. Randomly glue torn papers onto posterboard using gel medium applied with a foam brush. Let dry.

Body: Trace pattern pieces on collage. Cut out. • Punch 1/8" holes where indicated on pattern. Assemble body with brads or eyelets. Brads will allow joints to move. • Dress body with fabric, ribbons, silk flowers, and other embellishments. • Stamp face onto White cardstock. Cut out. Glue to smaller posterboard for added stability. Glue face on body, or glue photo to wood heart. Glue heart to body. Add hair if desired.

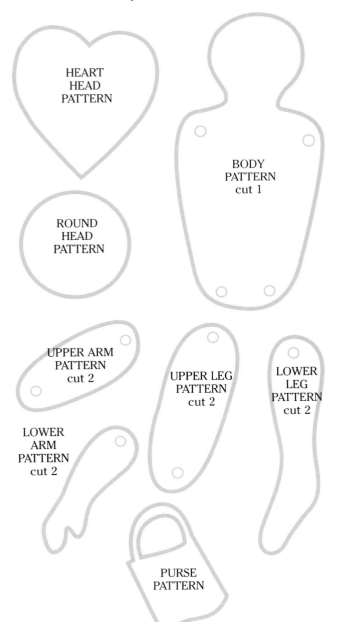

HEART HEAD PATTERN

BODY PATTERN cut 1

ROUND HEAD PATTERN

UPPER ARM PATTERN cut 2

UPPER LEG PATTERN cut 2

LOWER LEG PATTERN cut 2

LOWER ARM PATTERN cut 2

PURSE PATTERN

Paper Dolls

Here's a fun project for all paper doll lovers. Make several dolls with different faces and hair. Accessorize with hats, purses and different clothes. Spend a memorable afternoon making these dolls with your granddaughter or Girl Scout troop.

Flower Fairy

This pretty fairy gets her shape from a funnel. Use fabric scraps to bring this doll to life in your home.

"Flower Fairy"
- easy wrapped assembly
- no sewing
- rubber stamping on fabric
- stamped wings with little iron-on rhinestones

Products:
- stamps & inks
- red liner tape
- Lumiere paint (on funnel)
- wire
- beads

FINISHED SIZE: 8¹/₂" tall

MATERIALS:
Cotton fabric • Beads (Alphabet, leaf, flower) • Moss • 1 yd fibers • Dye based stamp pad • Permanent Black marker • *Hero Arts* flower stamp • 12 pipe cleaners • *Aleene's* Tacky glue • 22 gauge wire • Quilt batting • Lightweight cardboard • Color photocopy of face image • Heavy interfacing 2" x 6" for wings • *JudiKins* Diamond Glaze • Sponge • 6" plastic funnel • *Jacquard* Lumiere paint (Purple for funnel, Hair color for head)

INSTRUCTIONS:

Skirt: Apply 2 coats of Purple paint to funnel with sponge. • Stamp flower on three 8" x 12" fabric pieces with dye based ink. Tear into 1" x 12" strips. Remove fraying threads from edges. • Stack 3 strips of fabric. Fold in half. Lay a pipe cleaner into fold. Twist to secure layers together. Make 8 bundles. • Lay 4 bundles side by side. • Attach to one another using pipe cleaners to form waistband of first layer of skirt. Dab glue around neck of funnel, then wrap skirt around neck of funnel and twist pipe cleaners together to secure. Trim ends of pipe cleaners. • Repeat for second layer of skirt, wrap slightly higher on funnel neck than first skirt.

Neck/Head: Cut neck/head piece from cardboard. • Paint back of cardboard with Lumiere paint in color to match hair. Glue photocopy face image to front of cardboard. Glue hair to back of head. Insert neck end into funnel neck, secure with Tacky glue.

Arms: Twist 3 pipe cleaners together. • Wrap with thin layer of quilt batting. Wrap fabric strips around arms, covering batting. Secure end with glue. • Bend arms into a "U" shape. Place center of arms against neck. Attach by twisting wire around neck and arms.

Bodice: Cut quilt batting 2" x 5". Wrap batting around funnel neck. Glue in place. • Wrap 1" x 18" fabric strips around bodice and shoulders being sure to criss-cross and cover where arms are attached. Glue fabric ends in back.

Wings: Trace wings onto heavy interfacing with permanent Black marker. Color with Prismacolor pencils. Attach small crystals to wings with Diamond Glaze. • Glue wings to back of angel.

Decorations: Cut 22 gauge colored wire 12" long. Wrap 3" around left wrist. String alphabet beads to spell "flower". Make small coil in wire. Add "fairy" beads. • Wrap remaining wire around right wrist. • Glue Green moss, leaf, and flower bead embellishments at neck. • Wrap one yard of fibers around waist. Glue in place.

1. Fold skirt strip around pipe cleaner. Twist pipe cleaner closed.

2 Twist pipe cleaners together.

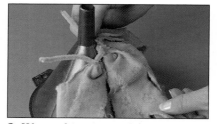

3. Wrap skirt around funnel.

4. Wrap top skirt around funnel.

5. Wrap bodice with fabric.

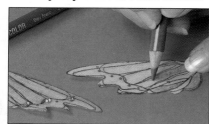

6. Color wings.

HEAD
PATTERN

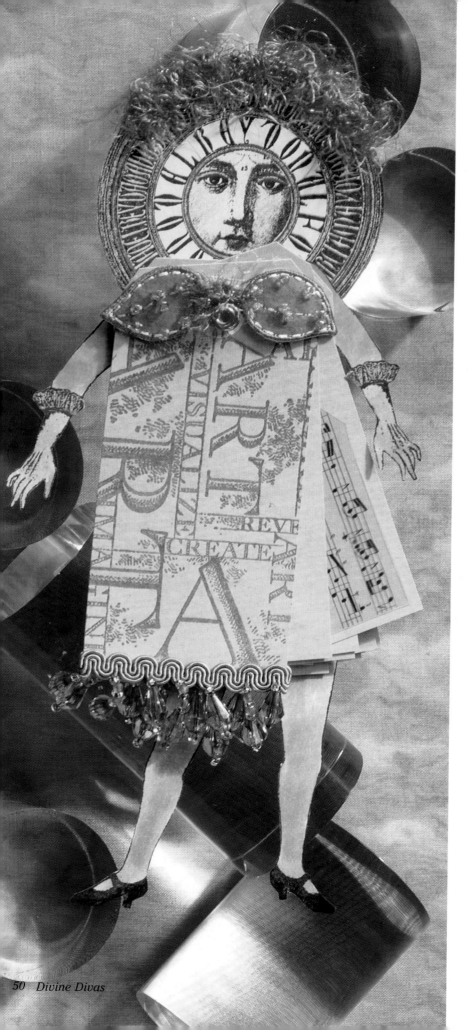

Doll Tag Book

Give up your ordinary memo pad. Have some fun taking this tag doll to the store with your grocery list. Or, collage some memorabilia onto the tags and set it on the coffee table for an unusual conversation piece.

FINISHED SIZE: 11" tall

MATERIALS:
Lightweight cardboard • *StazOn* Black ink pad • *Brilliance* Copper ink pad • Rubber stamps (*A Stamp In the Hand* Circle with Face; *Stampers Anonymous* U1-791 Art; *Character Constructions* #E-006) • Cream cardstock • *Prismacolor* pencils • Eyelets • Brads • 1 yd fuzzy fibers • 20 gauge Copper wire • *Tsukineko* (All Purpose Ink, Fantastix applicator) • Bead trim • Twelve #5 size shipping tags • *Marcel Schurman* Do-Jiggies leaves • Clear embossing powder • Red Liner tape • 1/8" hole punch • *Aleene's* Tacky glue

INSTRUCTIONS:
Face: Cut 3" circle of lightweight cardboard. • Stamp face onto Cream cardstock with Black ink. Color face using Prismacolor pencils. Cut out face. Glue to cardboard circle.

Hair: Punch 8 holes, 1/4" apart, along top edge of head. Set small eyelets. Wind one yard of fuzzy yarn through eyelets. Tie ends to secure. • Punch a hole below face. Set eyelet.

Cover: Stamp book cover with Copper stamp pad. Emboss with clear embossing powder. Attach row of bead trim to lower edge with Red Liner tape.

TAG
PATTERN